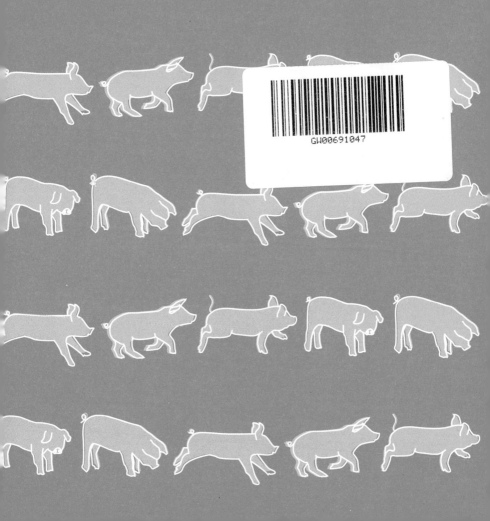

GW00691047

piglets at play

piglets at play

Sophie Bevan

photography by **Alan Williams**

RYLAND
PETERS
& SMALL

LONDON NEW YORK

Designer **Sarah Walden**

Editor **Sharon Ashman**

Location and Picture Researcher **Claire Hector**

Production **Patricia Harrington**

Art Director **Gabriella Le Grazie**

Publishing Director **Alison Starling**

First published in Great Britain in 2004
by Ryland Peters & Small
Kirkman House
12–14 Whitfield Street
London W1T 2RP
www.rylandpeters.com

10 9 8 7 6 5 4 3 2 1

Text, design and photographs
© Ryland Peters & Small 2004

ISBN 1 84172 613 3

A CIP record for this book is available from the
British Library.

Printed in China

contents

pigs on parade

pretty in pink

Pigs have had a lot of bad press. Their name has been considered synonymous with 'dirty', 'greedy', 'contrary', 'obstinate' and 'slobbish'. The time has come to put the record straight. The slander has to stop!

It simply isn't true that pigs are dirty. They may wallow in the mud to stay cool, but, as the ever-growing popularity of the house-pig proves, they're just as happy with a bit of luxury and proper air conditioning!

life in your hands

The truth is that the hog is a noble beast, whose service to mankind is too often unappreciated. The pig has been used for hunting game, for snuffling out truffles, for driving carts and for clearing land; he has been a soldier in battle and a loyal pet in peacetime. What's more, with advances in modern medicine, the pig now, quite literally, gives his heart to man.

a twist in the tail

an ancient line

The wild boar that can be recognized in early cave paintings may seem far removed from the cute little porker shown here. But black or pink, bristly or spotty, floppy-eared or razor-backed – pigs is pigs is pigs!

pigs on wall street

The pig was one of the first animals to be
domesticated by man, yet he was never one to
be tied to the house – or sty. In many parts of the
world pigs wander around freely, helping farmers
clear land by digging up roots. However, this
practice sometimes upsets the neighbours. On
Manhattan Island, seventeenth-century farmers
became so sick of rampaging pigs that they built
a wall to keep them out. The street running parallel
to the wall came to be known as Wall Street.

a twist in the tail

rootin' around

Today, we expect to encounter pigs rooting about in the woods for acorns. But years ago, the young pig-about-town was a common sight, too. In 1132, the French lost their heir to the throne – Prince Louis Philippe – in a fatal accident when his horse tripped over a piglet on a Parisian street. And across Europe, pigs belonging to St Anthony's hospitals have had special privileges to roam around the cities. These distinguished swine wore bells around their necks, and city dwellers became familiar with the ringing sound of a hungry pig outside their door.

Pigs were a common sight on city streets for several hundred years. In New York City, they were allowed to wander freely around the streets until the 1840s. And in Detroit it is still legal for pigs to roam, just as long as they have a ring in their nose to prevent them from foraging for roots.

'And there in a wood
a Piggy-wig stood,
With a ring at the end of his nose.'

Edward Lear, *The Owl and*
the Pussy Cat, 1845

On November 4, 1909, piglets officially took to the air. English eccentric Lord Brabazon cocooned our curly-tailed hero in a basket strapped to a wing strut of his biplane. The propellers were started, and Brabazon took his young charge on a 3½-mile ride through the clouds. The piglet was no doubt unimpressed by the experience, yet he proudly wore a sign telling all 'I am the first pig to fly'.

a twist in the tail

Not only masters of the air, pigs have also travelled the globe by sea. They were often kept on ships, where they ran about the decks as they pleased. They can be strong swimmers, too. One brave sow named 'Pig 311' was stationed on a US Navy ship in the South Pacific. Unappreciative of her military role, she dived into the sea and swam to safety on a nearby atoll, where she was rescued and taken back to the United States to live out her days at Washington Zoo.

'"The time has come," the Walrus said,
"To talk of many things:
Of shoes – and ships –
and sealing wax –
Of cabbages – and kings –
Of why the sea is boiling hot –
And whether pigs have wings."'

Lewis Carroll, *Through the Looking Glass*, 1872

this little piggy

farmyard hero

Grunting may not sound like the pinnacle of refined conversation, but that's not to say piglets aren't smart. The worthy pig has inspired great works of literature, has been depicted in priceless artworks and has played the hero in many a true tale.

this little piggy

fame at last

From Babe the sheep-pig to P. G. Wodehouse's Empress of Blandings (the fattest pig in all of Shropshire) and Napoleon in George Orwell's *Animal Farm*, the humble hog has graced the silver screen and the pages of great literature. Pigs have, on occasion, gone to great lengths for the sake of art. The famous artist Thomas Gainsborough brought live piglets into his house on Pall Mall in central London to 'sit' for his painting 'Girl with Pigs'. And Den-Den the Yorkshire pig is reported to have eaten 12 tubes of paint while having her celebrated portrait painted by James Wyeth.

dumb animals?

It should be no surprise to find that there's a lot going on between those big pink ears. Many animal psychologists rate pigs above dogs in terms of intelligence, and they can solve puzzles as quickly as the cleverest chimpanzee. Some young pigs have even been taught to use computer joysticks to adjust the temperature of their sties to suit their preferences.

In the late eighteenth century a craze for
'Learned Pigs' swept Europe and the United
States. These smart animals travelled from town
to town performing a range of tricks. In 1785
one celebrated porker even took to the stage
at Sadler's Wells theatre in London, amazing
his audience by telling the time and reading
people's minds. On the subject, Samuel Johnson
declared, '*Pig* has, it seems, not been wanting
to *man*, but *man* to *pig*. We do not allow time
for his education.'

It's clear that piglets are very special, and the many tales of piggy heroics back this up. In Roman times, pigs were sent into battle to frighten the elephants that were often used by invading armies. During the English Civil War, a hog saved the besieged city of Gloucester – he was marched around the city walls, squealing all the way, to convince Royalist enemies that the city still had plenty of supplies. And, more recently, in 1983 a particularly brave sow named Priscilla rescued a drowning boy from a lake in Texas.

this little piggy

*'Day after day my lessons fade,
My intellect gets muddy;
A trough I have, and not a desk,
A stye and not a study!'*

Thomas Hood, *The Lament of Toby, the Learned Pig,*

1835

piggy pals

pigs and whistles

Piglets are curious creatures, always interested in new sights, sounds – and smells! If you're passing a field of pigs, it's likely that you'll rouse some interest, especially from friendly piglets, always looking to play.

When piglets have been out rooting and gambolling in the fields, their owners need to call them in at the end of the day. What you might think requires merely a 'here, pig!' has developed into quite an art form, with hog-calling contests drawing great crowds at shows all over the United States.

'S-o-o-o-u-u-u-e-e-e-y!'

Traditional hog call

Pigs have a remarkable sense of smell and were first trained to sniff out truffles in the sixteenth century in France, where they are still employed today. Sows are accompanied by their piglets who are expected to 'learn on the job'. Of course, pigs know a good thing when they smell it, so they have to be muzzled to stop them gorging themselves on the valuable fungi.

piggy bank

The family pig has long been valued. In Ireland
he was referred to as 'the gentleman who pays the
rent'. And in ancient China, around the end
of the first millennium, pigs were so revered that
prominent individuals would be buried with
life-sized ceramic models of their pigs. Today,
the pig has found his rightful place as an important
member of many families, living in the house
alongside his owners and playing the devoted
pet as well as any dog could.

While most house-pigs are doted on and lavished with everything a piglet could want, this hasn't always been the case. In the court of King Louis XI of France, piglets were expected to sing for their supper. Apparently the king was prone to dark moods, which could only be lifted by singing, dancing pigs. The unlucky troop was dressed in wigs and gowns, and paraded through the palace.

'Never teach a pig to sing. It wastes your time and annoys the pig.'

Traditional saying

piggy pals

55

Luckily, these happy pigs are free to squeal and grunt as and when they please. In today's farmyards it's the pigs who are given the entertainment. In Europe it is advised that all pigs are provided with toys in their sties. These range from balls and chains to plastic piping and logs – while across the Atlantic, the privileged pigs at the Pennsylvania State University get to play with special computer games and their success is rewarded with sweets!

swine fever

In the past 20 years, the popularity of pet pigs has boomed. These aren't just hick hogs – some of these pets live at the best Beverly Hills addresses, and can be seen trotting after their owners down Rodeo Drive. Pigs are smart, clean, loving and loyal. They enjoy playing a game of fetch, and are in hog heaven curled up for a cuddle on a warm lap. And if anyone tells you that's hogwash – they just don't know pigs!

'That's all Folks!'

Porky Pig (1935–)

'So she set the little creature down, and felt quite relieved to see it trot away quietly into the wood. "If it had grown up," she said to herself, "it would have made a dreadfully ugly child: but it makes rather a handsome pig, I think." And she began thinking over other children she knew, who might do very well as pigs ...'

Lewis Carroll, *Alice's Adventures in Wonderland,*

1865

acknowledgments

The publisher would like to thank all those who helped with the photography for this book:

Odds Farm Park, High Wycombe, Buckinghamshire, Amazing Animals and Pig Paradise, Derbyshire.

Special thanks to our human models Tom, Katie and Emily and to Tony York of Pig Paradise for all his help and advice.

Pig Paradise
Blackfordby Hall
Blackfordby
Derbyshire
DE11 8AB
www.pigparadise.com
Special one-day courses on rare breed pigs, rearing traditional pig breeds and pig keeping.

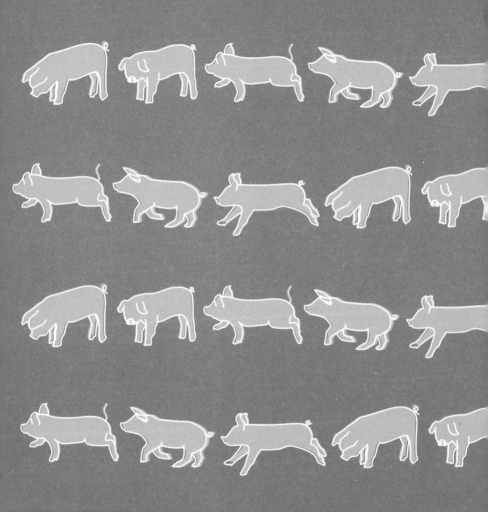